Celebrating YOU

It's Your Birthday!

__ __ __ __ __ __
Month   Day   Year

By Wendy English

Copyright © 2023 Wendy English.
All rights reserved. ISBN: 979-8-9864106-2-3
Fonts and graphics licensed through
Canva & Creative Market

Dedicated to my best friend, Penny, who makes every birthday so much fun! May you know what an incredible joy you are to all who know you and what a treasure your life is too!

*How many green birds can you find in this book?

Pick your cake,
and candles too

*How many candles will be on your cake?

It's time to celebrate...
amazing you!

*which one is your favorite balloon?

Pick balloons, the best you've seen,

yellow, blue and green.

And now it's time to pick your hat,

and open your
presents too!

Remember to say

thanks,

Thanks!

*Pick the balloons you would give to your friends!

and give balloons
to your friends,

then play a game
or two!

Next it's time to make a wish,

and sing a little tune.

La La La

La La La

Be sure to thank
God above,
as they sing
happy birthday...

Tape your photo here!

to you!

Happy Birthday!

*Color in this special verse!

"For I know the plans I have for you," declares the Lord, "Plans to prosper you and not to harm you, plans to give you hope and a future."

Jeremiah 29:11

www.ingramcontent.com/pod-product-compliance
Lightning Source LLC
Chambersburg PA
CBHW051619010526
44119CB00008B/203